W0007768

ABOVE: *Making potato baskets in Wales in the 1930s. These are typical frame baskets. The shape is formed by a skeleton of split hazel and the weaving is of willow.*

COVER: *The author, Alastair Heseltine, at work making a basket.*

BASKETS AND
BASKETMAKING

Alastair Heseltine

Shire Publications Ltd

CONTENTS

Set in 10 on 9 point Times roman and printed in Great Britain by C. I. Thomas & Sons (Haverfordwest) Ltd, Press Buildings, Merlins Bridge, Haverfordwest.

Copyright © 1982 by Alastair Heseltine. First published 1982; reprinted 1986, 1990. Shire Album 92. ISBN 0 85263 611 3.

All rights reserved. No part of this publication may be reproduced or transmitted in any form or by any means, electronic or mechanical, including photocopy, recording, or any information storage and retrieval system, without permission in writing from the publishers, Shire Publications Ltd, Cromwell House, Church Street, Princes Risborough, Buckinghamshire HP17 9AJ, UK.

ACKNOWLEDGEMENTS

The author wishes to thank Martyn Brown and David Drew for specially preparing photographs; Dorothy Wright and Christopher Coate for their aid with the script; and Jean Heseltine for doing all the typing.

Photographs are acknowledged as follows: Urdd Gobaith Cymru, page 1; Institute of Agricultural History and Museum of English Rural Life, University of Reading, pages 3, 5 (bottom), 6 (top), 13, 28, 29 (top); Luton Museum and Art Gallery, page 5 (top); Lincolnshire Libraries, Grantham, pages 5 (centre), 10 (top); Somerset Rural Life Museum, pages 9, 10 (bottom left), 11 (both), 15, 17 (both), 18 (both), 19 (top left and right), 21 (top), 22 (top), 23, 24 (bottom); Commercial Camera Craft, Yeovil, page 12; Fernand de Vos, page 8. The lower photograph on page 31 is reproduced by kind permission of Margaret Foster and was first published in *Bygone Kent*.

A 'swill' made from oak that has been split, boiled and torn by hand into thin strips of spale. The manufacture of frame baskets of this kind was once a local industry in Cumbria.

'Corves' were used in the mines to haul both miners and coal up the shafts. They were made from coppiced hazel.

INTRODUCTION

Baskets have always been popular and familiar and they are therefore often taken for granted. Nowadays when almost everything is machine manufactured it is seldom realised that all baskets are entirely made by hand and that basketmaking is a profession. For the most part those available in the shops are cheap, light and commercial. They are made in countries outside Europe where they are mass-produced on moulds to give the uniformity required by importers. The baskets once in use on farms and in industry all over Britain were not like this. They were sturdy and functional and made in Britain by craftsmen using native materials such as willow (this is entirely different to *cane*, which comes from the Far East). A small number of traditional craftsmen still work today and willow is still grown specially for basketmaking, mainly in the West Country. The following account explains what goes on in a profession that has remained fundamentally unchanged for centuries.

HISTORY

The art of basketmaking was developed at an early stage of man's evolution. In Britain oak, hazel and willow provided material for making the strong rigid containers necessary in everyday life. Fences and houses, too, were built from *wickerwork* or *wattles*. Early baskets were probably much like those found in the farms of highland regions until the second half of the twentieth century. 'Frame' baskets were constructed with wild materials on simple but time-consuming principles, and in these areas basketmaking mostly remained a seasonal job reserved for the dark days of winter. In lowland Britain the weaving of willow, using different techniques, developed into a profession and ultimately a sizable industry. The number of craftsmen employed and the output of their labours must have been immense, but such are the temporary nature of willow and the humble status of the basketmaker that the evidence of the scale of production has all but disappeared. In practically every instance where today one needs cardboard, plastic or plywood for packing material, two hundred years ago this need would have been met by wickerwork. Fruit and vegetables were gathered from the fields into baskets; fish, poultry and dairy produce were all packed into wicker for the journey to the town markets. Jobs requiring the transport of bulky materials such as manure or rubble needed baskets, and not only were rural items such as animal muzzles, bird traps and beer strainers made of willow, but so were the travelling trunks, hat boxes and umbrella holders of the well-to-do.

The distribution of workshops depended on local demand and favourable conditions for growing willows. In certain counties these factors combined to create a concentration of makers, often within a small area of several villages. At the beginning of the twentieth century East Anglia and the East Midlands, the plain of York, Worcestershire, Gloucestershire, Kent, Bedfordshire and the Thames Valley supported a fair number of country workshops, making for the most part simple agricultural baskets. A greater variety of produce was to be found in the important centres of Lancashire, Somerset and the Trent Valley (Nottinghamshire and Leicestershire), while the largest and most sophisticated workshops were found in the towns. Guilds of basketmakers were formed. Records show that the Worshipful Company of Basketmakers of the City of London was established before 1469. This company was eventually granted a royal charter by George VI in 1937, but by then its old responsibilities had long since been taken on by the trade unions.

Decline of the basket trade has continued throughout the twentieth century for many economic reasons. An economy in which time has much value and quality very little has no place for a durable product that is extremely labour-intensive. Moreover, where the use of wicker has still been viable, the cheapness of foreign labour has often led to basket importation. British basketmakers, as members of an industrially advanced country, started to experience the undermining of their trade in the second half of the nineteenth century. Imports from the Netherlands, Germany and France severely affected the makers of agricultural work up to 1939. Wartime renewed the demand for baskets but since then competition in the domestic market has continued from the products of Spain, Eastern Bloc countries such as Poland, and the Far East. Consequently between 1945 and 1980 the number of 'twiggies' (as some makers call themselves) fell from seven thousand to about five hundred, of whom two hundred were blind and working under subsidised conditions. Today accomplished basketmakers are few. The blind workshops still produce articles of a robust nature superior in strength to importations, although not necessarily very refined. In comparison many other makers, in attempts to beat importation on the same ground, have taken short cuts and generally lost the merits and quality of traditional willow work.

RIGHT: *A seed lip in Luton Museum made from split ash and willow. The type of construction, called 'scuttle work', is incredibly durable but is now a lost art.*

LEFT: *An excerpt from the trade catalogue of William Harrison of Grantham, Lincolnshire, showing a wicker invalid chair.*

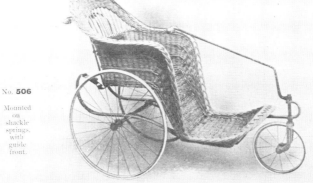

No. **506**

Mounted on shackle springs, with guide front.

A 14in. seat, with 25in. and 12in. ⅜ wired-on tyred wheels,

B 16in. seat, with 25in. and 12in. ⅜ wired-on tyred wheels.

C 18in. seat, with 26in. and 12in. ¾ wired-on tyred wheels,

92/- **110/-** **126/-**

RIGHT: *An eel trap made from white willow. The eels enter at the flared end through a funnel of willow that prevents return. The neck is plugged with a wooden stopper.*

5

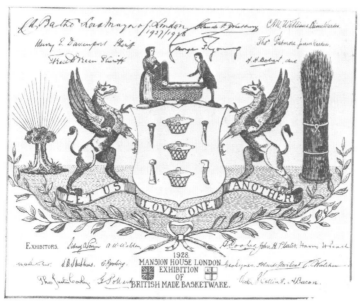

LEFT: *The arms of the Worshipful Company of Basketmakers of the City of London.*

MINERS MARK BASKET, LIGHT RANDED, ROUND.

10″ dia. Bottom, 15″ dia. Top, 13″ Deep I.S.M., 5½ B.S., 22 Stakes, 2 Handles, 4 rounds Upsett, 2 rounds Top Waling, 2 Border Bands, 5 round Bands on Upsett. If made with 2 Centre Wales. Extra Charge. .... 5s. 0d.

ONE GALLON STONE JARS, COARSE SLEWED.

4½ B.S., 15 Stakes, 2 rounds Upsett, 2 Single Rod Handles on Border. Nozzle tied on with one tie, Cane Loop for Hasp, Twisted Cane Noose.

With Cap .... 2s. 9½d.
Without Cap .... 2s. 1½d.

OIL CAN BASKETS, BROWN SLEWED.

Gallons	Dia. Bottom	Depth	B.S.	Stakes	s.	d.
1	—	—	—	—	2	6
2	9¾″	16″	5½	21	3	5½
5	12½″	23″	5½	21	4	4

3 rounds Upsett, 2 rounds Top Waling, Randed Bottom, 2 Double Rod Handles on Border of 2 × 5 Gallons. One on Small Size.

OVAL CLOTHES BASKET, LIGHT RANDED (STRONG).

23″ × 15″ Bottom, 30″ × 23″ Top, 13″/15″ Deep I.S.M., 4 Layer Open, 4 on ends, 40 Stakes, 3 rounds Upsett, 1 round Top Waling,

RIGHT: *Extract from the last issue of the 'National List of Basic Wage Rates in the Basket Industry' (1956). The unions developed strict rules of costing on a piecework system, but the regulations laid down in the 'Red Book', as it was known, were largely ignored in country areas.*

6

Hand cutting of willow rods in Somerset. A skilled man can cut forty bundles a day and an acre (0.4 ha) a week.

WILLOW CULTIVATION

Willow must have been cultivated for almost as long as it has been used for basketmaking. The readiness with which a small branch pushed into soil will take root and send out shoots undoubtably lent itself to exploitation by man at an early period. While Pliny (AD 23 — 79) gives the first historical instance of osier growing, it is only within recent times that cultivation has been commercial or to any degree scientific. Until the nineteenth century *willow garths*, or *withy beds*, were collections of mixed varieties in which the growing plants were cut off at several feet allowing a head of shoots to spring from a single stem or *stool*. Old beds on this system still exist in places, the stools standing several feet apart above weeds and most animals. The shoots are cut off and are known as *osiers, withies* in the West Country, or simply *rods*. To obtain rods that are straight and clean of branches all developments of this system have favoured cutting the stool back as near as possible to ground level. In modern withy beds there is little visible

after the harvest except a knotty mass underfoot. It is hard to imagine that this can grow every year into a forest of green rods and leaves higher than a man.

Several hundreds of varieties of willow have been selected over the centuries, often with curious names: 'Trustworthy', 'Swallowtail', 'Whissender', 'Mealy Top', 'Dicky Meadowes'. Many consist of the species *Salix viminalis*, or common osier, and its crosses: they tend to produce a vigorous growth suitable for heavy coarse baskets. Finer quality material is obtained from *Salix triandra*, or almond-leafed willow, and today nearly all basket willows grown in Britain are of this species, the majority of which are the variety 'Black Maul'.

Present-day cultivation is almost entirely concentrated within the flat lowland moors surrounding the rivers Parret, Tone and Isle in Somerset. Blocks of withies up to 10 acres (4 ha), divided by drainage ditches and interspersed with rough pasture, give the area a characteristic atmosphere. The land has a high water table and is liable to occasional floods, excluding most agriculture, but at the same time the topsoil is fertile and normally well drained, which is ideal for willows. It is a misconception that swampy conditions are favourable; the best rods grow on good land.

Beds are established by planting 9 to 12 inch (23 to 30 cm) lengths of willow cut from the thick ends of good-sized rods. A large number are needed (sometimes over thirty thousand per acre) and each is pushed into the soil by hand in lines spaced to accommodate machinery. To establish a healthy bed the land must be clean of weeds and frequently cultivated during the first two years. After this time, as crops become successively denser, the foliage tends to keep down competition, but weed control remains necessary. If well managed a bed can last over fifty years.

Attention must be given throughout the growing season to ensure a crop that is usable for basketmaking: any damage at the very tender growing point produces an unsalable branched rod. Frost in May is the first hazard so cattle are grazed in the beds to hold back all growth until the danger is past. Later in the season hail, fungoid diseases and insect attacks can all do serious damage. Towards the end of summer growth stops at a height around 7 feet (2 m) and the wood matures. Cutting can begin after leaf fall, which is usually in early November following frost.

Many willows are still cut by hand, a skilled and laborious occupation that can last all winter. A heavy hook is used and the cutter bends double in order to cut as low and cleanly as possible. He is paid piece-rate on the number of bundles cut and tied up, each having a circumference of 3 feet 2 inches (97 cm) at the base. A yield of about two hundred bundles to the acre is hoped for. Since 1979 more and more willows are being harvested by a machine invented by a Belgian grower. The machine cuts and ties, greatly reducing the manual labour.

The cutting machine made in Belgium by Fernand de Vos can cut and bind 2½ acres (1 ha) a day.

Mr L. Musgrove of Westonzoyland with willows drying for browns. It takes until spring before the sap begins to dry out. The bundles are occasionally turned to prevent any heating or fermentation.

WILLOW PROCESSING

There is much work to be done before the willow passes into the hands of the basket-maker. The crop is hauled to the yard for sorting. The bundles are opened and the rods stood upright in a barrel against a measuring stick. Starting with the longest, they are drawn out by the handful and graded into sizes by the foot length; grass, weeds and material below 2 feet (60 cm) remain at the bottom and are discarded. Then each grade is bundled separately into *wads* of about 2 feet 7 inches (79 cm) circumference. The fresh wads are heavy and being full of sap are known as *greens*. A certain proportion will be dried outside and sold as *browns*. These words do not necessarily refer to the colour of the rods, which depends on variety and soil conditions; in Somerset 'brown' Black Maul has a green bark slightly mottled with black.

While browns are rather rough for basketmaking, the removal of the bark by

stripping or *peeling* provides a material altogether different and more refined. Most of the crop is sold stripped following one of two different processes. Stripping *whites* takes place within a limited season. The wads of withies are kept living by being stood upright in several inches of water; this is known as *pitting*. At the end of April as the sap rises and buds break, the skin no longer adheres to the wood and can be pulled off in one, leaving a shiny white rod. Once all withies were stripped by being pulled one by one through a hand *brake* but now machines are used; this is much faster but none the less hard work. Whitening can be continued until a second year's wood starts to form in July but sometimes willows cut in April are stripped directly without any pitting, in which case there is only about a week to finish the job.

Stripping *buffs* can take place at any time of the year and present-day growers prefer to produce this way in order to

9

ABOVE: *Stripping for whites near Spalding, Lincolnshire, c 1910. In the days of hand brakes women and children were required to complete the job within the season. In Somerset the schools stopped for several weeks.*
BELOW RIGHT: *A simple hand brake for stripping willows made from $\frac{1}{2}$ inch (13 mm) sprung steel and about 2 feet (60 cm) long. The brake is mounted upright and the willow pulled between the two jaws.*
BELOW LEFT: *Machine stripping in Somerset. A handful of willows is held against banks of brakes fixed to a rotating drum. One man can strip forty wads a day.*

spread the workload; the skin comes away more easily too. The wads are packed into large tanks of water, covered and boiled from eight to ten hours. Stripping follows while the rods are still warm. Buffing was first devised in 1860 in order to obtain the now familiar light chestnut colour. Originally the experimenters boiled the rods in urine, but it is the tannins naturally present in the willow that are responsible for dyeing the wood, and it was found that clean water produces the same results, with the added benefit of a strong, pleasant, aromatic smell.

After stripping both whites and buffs must be dried, and it is common to see them spread out against the fences in the wind. Drying sheds are also used, especially in winter. The dried rods are finally tied up into sale bundles, called *bolts*, made up from about two wads. A bundle is priced irrespective of length and is considered rather like a unit of value by growers and basketmakers. Tying with two withies twisted into *bonds* is in itself quite an art. A bundle should be tight and neat with a 3 feet 1 inch (94 cm) circumference at a point 2 inches (5 cm) from the *butts,* that is the thick ends, of the withies.

Although the willow grower was often the basketmaker, the two occupations are now almost entirely separated. There is

ABOVE: *Willows drying against a fence.*

BELOW: *Wads of willows about to be boiled for buff. In this case a steel cage facilitates loading. The tank is oil-fired.*

some advantage for the maker in being able to purchase a professionally produced and standardised material, but at the same time his choice is often limited, especially when dependent on road and rail delivery. The sort of material (generally referred to as *stuff*) he can expect for sale in the present day is bolts of buff, white and brown withies from 8 feet to 4 and sometimes 3 feet (1 foot = 30.5 cm). Within a bundle. of 6 feet for example, only a proportion of rods will be to full length while the remainder will vary down to 5 feet. The thin ends or *tops* should be fine and not crushed or forked, nor should there be any black patches, which denote fungus damage. A light dusting of mould is not harmful. A strong orange buff from winter boiling has inferior working qualities to a shiny golden buff from summer boiling. *Sticks* are willows of two or more years for making square work and handles. They can be buffed or whited and are sometimes sold by weight. When they are not available makers sometimes use pollard willows and woodland hazels. The approximate weights of bundles are: 4 feet, 17 pounds; 5 feet, 20 pounds; 6 feet, 24 pounds; 7 feet, 28 pounds. The average price per bundle of buffs, whites and browns in 1986 was £10.50, £12 and £8 respectively.

Tying up a bundle of stripped rods.

Making 'pot' hampers at Cleveload, Worcestershire, in 1937. The hampers were produced in thousands for agricultural use. Eight a day used to be the craftsman's target.

THE WORKSHOP

The basketmaker is fortunate in that his workshop and equipment require very little outlay. A small collection of hand tools and enough room to work a 7-foot willow are the only real essentials. There are many individual craftsmen, often part-time or retired, who work satisfactorily in back rooms and garden sheds. More established workshops are usually simple and bare to avoid obstruction of the rapidly moving rods. If there is enough space all half-opened bundles of rods, sticks and accompanying muddle are kept outside or away from the working position of the maker, namely his *plank*.

The plank is simply wooden boards about 5 feet 6 inches by 2 feet 6 inches (170 by 80 cm), resting on the ground to provide a level and dry workplace amidst the willow. The basketmaker sits at one end, back to the wall, with perhaps his tool box or a cushion to lean upon, so he is almost at ground level. On the floor each side are his rods; his tools are to his right, while the basket in front is inclined away from him on the *lapboard*. This position enables him to keep the willows neat and ready at hand; it maintains the humidity of his material and thus his efficiency. Humidity is of importance since willow is worked damp and should it dry it will return to a brittle state. Centrally heated houses do not provide the best workshop conditions, nor unfortunately on dry sunny

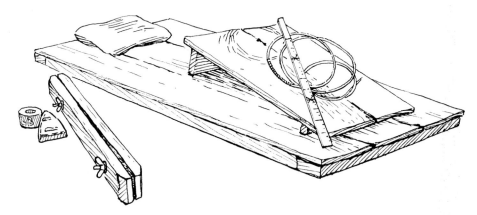

days do open doors and windows. Efficient working outdoors with stripped rods is impossible. This may explain why many traditional workshops are rather dank and dismal, but then too the basketmaker has often had to make do with humble premises. Above all things the scent of the willow gives a characteristic atmosphere. White, brown and buff rods each have a distinctive fresh smell of their own, while offcuts and old material underfoot give a musty odour. Wasted material is inevitable and in some workshops is allowed to mount up in quantity, which, it has been explained, 'keeps the place warm in winter'.

The essential tool kit consists of a *shop knife*, secateurs or *shears*, a *beating iron* for knocking down the weaving, and a steel *bodkin* for piercing holes. For squarework both a *commander* to straighten sticks and a *screw-block* to hold them upright while making bottoms are necessary. Only the first two items can still be purchased although all are simple enough to be blacksmith-made; most makers rely on well used equipment handed down through several generations. Other tools are more specialised. While shears are often used for trimming up finished work, the cleanest method is with a *pick knife*. Split rods, or *skeins*, for binding purposes, are split and planed down in thickness and width by *cleave*, *shave* and *upright* respectively. A *shell bodkin* is good for passing a frayed top through an awkward place.

The only item of any expense for a well equipped workshop is a trough of water at least 7 feet (2 m) long. This is essential for soaking browns or any quantity of buffs or whites.

ABOVE: *The basketmaker's plank, lapboard and essential improvised equipment, including a yardstick, hoops of various sizes, screw blocks, and weights for stabilising baskets.*

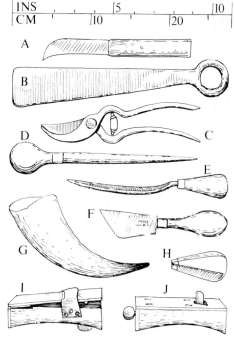

ABOVE: *A, shop knife; B, beating iron combined with commander (the ring end), weight about ¼ pound (200 g); C, shears; D, bodkin; E, shell bodkin; F, pick knife; G, grease horn for greasing bodkins; H, three-way cleave; I, shave; J, upright.*

14

BASKETMAKING

Although under union ruling three years of apprenticeship, and at least one of improvership, were necessary to become a basketmaker, serviceable baskets can be produced after very little instruction. The basic technical details are simple, yet at the same time it is often said among basketmakers that one never stops learning because, as in all crafts, real knowledge is gained at a physical level and only through experience. Fluency and productivity cannot be learnt immediately. The following account describes the sort of work involved in the production of a round general purpose farm basket of the sort sold nowadays for logs. This basket is known regionally as a 'kipe', 'skep' or 'butt', and while being of the simplest design it combines all the fundamentals of traditional basketwork.

The description is intended to be complete enough to be used as instruction for

A withy butt.

amateurs, but it may be found that the size of the willows in this example is too great for unskilled hands. Smaller baskets with smaller willows can be made on exactly the same principle, such as the fruit picker illustrated on page 25.

SOAKING UP

Willow is stored dry but to be made pliable it must be soaked in water. In order to start the day with well prepared material the basketmaker usually *soaks up* his stuff the evening before. For a daily production of four log baskets he ties about one third of a bundle of 6 foot (180 cm) and one half of a bundle of 8 foot (240 cm) into wads and immerses them in the water tank for about an hour; then he removes them to a cool draught-free place to lie and *mellow.* Mellowing means allowing surface water to penetrate uniformly right through to the pith for several hours; overnight is ideal. In the morning the rods are damp, cool and sweet-smelling, but not wet or slippery.

He arranges the longest wads alongside the left of the plank and the smallest to the right, butts towards the wall. Kept neatly they will be in good working condition all day, but muddled or left lying too long, especially when warm, they will dry out or develop a greasy mould which makes work slow and unpleasant. Each morning therefore the basketmaker first uses up any stuff left over from the day before and in the evening he takes care to judge accurately his needs for the next day. Soaking-up time varies depending on the hardness and variety of willow, but the following table is a guide for Somerset Black Maul:

	5 *foot*	7 *foot*
buffs and whites	¾ hour	1 hour
browns	5 days	7 days

Water temperature too makes a difference: warm conditions can hasten the soaking of browns by several days. Browns are best drained off and mellowed for about a day before use. The maker without a tank soaks and mellows stripped stuff *in situ* by cover-

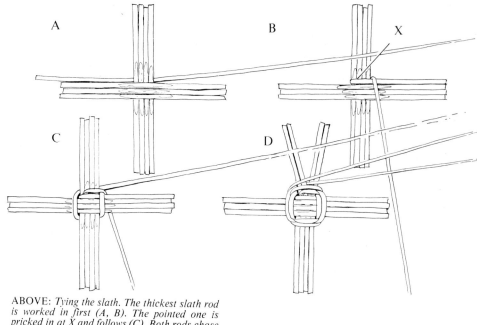

A

B

X

C

D

ABOVE: *Tying the slath. The thickest slath rod is worked in first (A, B). The pointed one is pricked in at X and follows (C). Both rods chase round two or three times, then start to open out (D).*

RIGHT: *A bottom stick slyped in the belly. A slype is a long cut with the shop knife. The belly is the concave side. The back of a stick or rod is the convex side.*

ing the rods with sacks and watering them liberally.

TYING THE SLATH

The *slath* is the central structure of a round or oval bottom. From the opened bundle of 8 foot to his left he selects twenty-eight of the thickest rods and with his secateurs cuts 16 inches (40 cm) off each butt end. These are the *bottom sticks*, enough for four baskets. He *slypes* each shallowly in the *belly*. He picks out four thickish 6 foot and four thinner, slyping the latter to a point at the butt ends with a single knife stroke. These are his *slath rods*. Taking one of each and seven bottom sticks, he proceeds to tie the slath underfoot in the pattern illustrated, with firm tight strokes.

PAIRING

Now he *opens out* the bottom sticks with the pair of slath rods, first in doubles, then singly, like the spokes of a wheel, and once this has begun the slath becomes a stable unit that will not fly undone. Holding the work beneath the left foot, one slath rod after the other is worked behind consecutive bottom sticks until both run out at the tops. The stroke is called pairing.

To join in fresh rods the maker selects a pair from the smaller stuff to his right. He lays the tops into the weaving where the slath rods finish and continues pairing as before. All subsequent rods are started by the butts. The rough ends are left sticking up on the side facing the maker, which will eventually become the underneath of the basket. To give structure and solidity he pulls the bottom sticks towards him to create a saucer shape and tightly packs the weaving down with the left hand and an occasional tap from the iron. Finally, when a 14 inch (35 cm) diameter is reached, he secures the last pair of tops by pulling them through the weaving. All four bottoms are completed and the projecting bottom sticks trimmed flush to the circumference before continuing.

ABOVE: *Tying the slath.*
BELOW: *Opening out.*

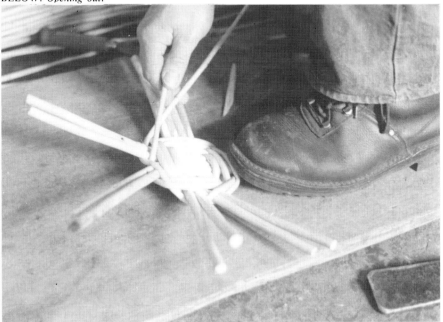

17

ABOVE: *Pairing.*
BELOW: *Staking up.*

18

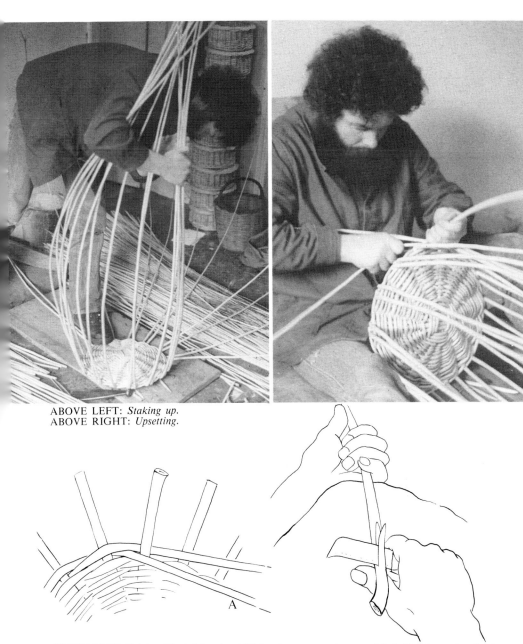

ABOVE LEFT: *Staking up.*
ABOVE RIGHT: *Upsetting.*

A

ABOVE LEFT: *Pairing. The left-hand rod (A) is taken over one bottom stick, behind the next and out again. All basket strokes progress from left to right.*
ABOVE RIGHT: *Slyping a stake on the back. The left wrist rests tightly behind the left knee, and the cut is made towards the maker. Maximum force is safely exerted this way.*

19

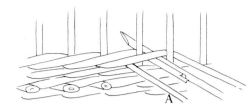

LEFT: *Three-rod waling. The left-hand rod (A) is taken over two stakes and behind one. Note the joining of butt to butt and the broken* **rod.**

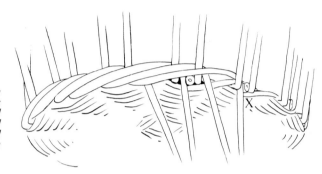

RIGHT: *Four-rod pull-down wale. The left-hand rod is taken over three stakes and behind one. Every second stroke is pulled down hard between the stake and bottom stick (X).*

STAKING UP

The remaining 8 foot rods are slyped to a sharp point on the back at the butt. These rods are called *stakes* and will form the uprights and border of the basket. Standing inside the concave face of the bottom, he takes twenty-nine of them. One by one they are grasped in his left hand, belly facing up, and driven alongside each side of each bottom stick by a hammer blow of his right fist. This makes fourteen pairs of stakes and one single one driven in at the place where the bottom sticks appear closest. Now he turns the spider-like structure over and kinks the stakes one by one through 90 degrees while turning the point of his knife into the pith to avoid any breakage. This is known as *pricking up*. Once pricked, he gathers them together and passes them through a hoop of about 15 inches (40 cm) diameter, which secures them in the ultimate form of the basket. The hoop is itself secured by a stake bent down and curled around it.

UPSETTING

The first rounds of weaving are called the *upset*. They control the ultimate shape of the basket, give solidity and in this case form the bottom edge. *Waling* is the stroke used. The maker may now sit down. First, with the 'basket' lying in front of him, he uses his iron to beat the shoulders formed where the stakes are pricked up level with the ends of the bottom sticks; then, pointing four of the 6 foot at the butt he sticks, or *pricks*, each into the bottom to the left of four consecutive stakes to weave a *four-rod pull-down wale*. He begins two sets of this wale in diametrically opposite places and where the one meets the other cuts off one of the four rods and continues to climb with a three wale. The basket is now placed upright on the lapboard, sometimes pinned by a bodkin, and stabilised by a weight inside. After the preliminary rods are finished he starts further wales by the tops, works to the butts and joins butt to butt with another three rods. In this way he keeps the upset even by waling sets of six rods.

SIDING UP

With the hoop removed the stakes spring out in a regular form. The maker pencil-marks several stakes at 19 inches (48 cm)

20

ABOVE: *Siding up.*

Slewing. The willows are staggered, those above in advance. When a top is run out underneath, a new rod is laid in above maintaining a continuous packet of three or more. Systems using a single rod are called 'randing'.

from the lapboard and checks that the diameter at this height will be 20 inches (50 cm). Then he grades to length any tops cut from the previous basket and some 6 foot. Taking always the shortest material first, he starts *slewing*. This system of *siding up* is dependent on an odd number of stakes. His left thumb pushes the slew behind the stake; his right hand catches it. Tops are left outside, butts laid inside. His left fist repeatedly beats the weaving even. At the top he puts on a set of three-rod wale, using the rods from which the bottom sticks were cut, and beats it down level to the pencil mark with his iron.

It will be apparent to anybody following this description that willow does not always neatly respond to the patterns illustrated and, unlike cane, tends to kink permanently in awkward places. Kinks should only occur where the rods lie against the stakes, which themselves must remain straight and even. This requires skill and force.

BORDERING OFF

The top is finished by kinking down the stakes to make a 'five behind two' border. Should they have started to dry out, at least a dip in water will be necessary to avoid breaking at this point. On completion the maker trims away the border tops, to be used later as slewing, and *picks off* all other protruding butts and tops with his pick knife or secateurs, leaving the cut ends lying against the stakes. The four baskets are finished and stacked up awaiting handles.

21

ABOVE: *Bordering off.*

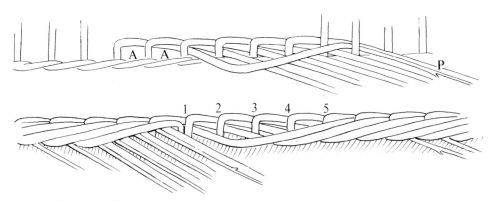

ABOVE: *Five-rod border. Five stakes are kinked down behind two, forming five tops. Each stroke consists of taking the left-hand top over four stakes and behind the fifth while the next stake is brought down with it, forming a pair (P). Five pairs are formed; the left-hand rod in each pair is abandoned. To finish, both tops and stakes are pulled through at A while the five remaining tops are kinked, slyped and 'crammed' down against the stakes (1 to 5) they would normally go behind. The first cram is shown already in position at 1.*

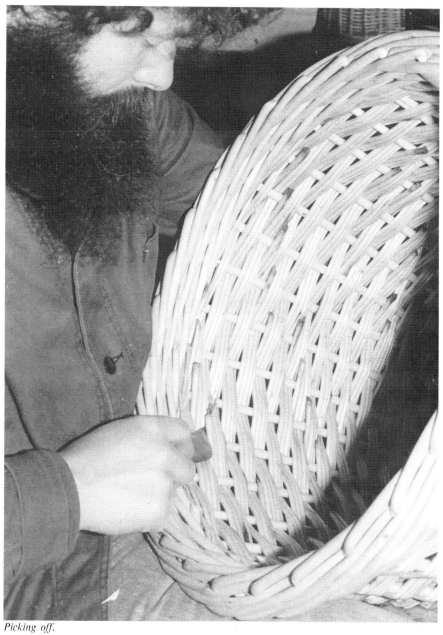

Picking off.

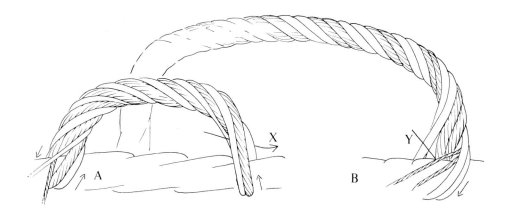

ABOVE: *Rope handles. (A) Lug handle seen from the inside. The last turn of the bow rod (shaded) does not go under the wale but turns back round the bow at X. Both tops end on the left. (B) Cross handle made on an inch-thick stick bow. Two 7 foot rods (shaded) are pricked beside the bow, (Y) lapped five times around, passed under the wale the other side and returned to Y. Two more rods (unshaded) repeat the pattern from the other side.*

LEFT: *Handling.*

24

A fruit picker made on exactly the same principles as the log basket described. The number of bottom sticks is five, and the bottom is 9 inches in diameter. There are twenty-one stakes from 7 foot, slewed with tops, and 5 foot to 11½ inches, with 14 inches diameter. There is a five-rod border, and a cross handle made on a stick driven into the slewing.

HANDLING

With one foot inside the basket he pricks in two stout 8 foot about 6 inches apart down through the border alongside the stakes. He forces a hole under the wale with his bodkin and pulls the left rod through from the outside, forming a smooth *bow* three fingers' width from the border. Then he twists the right rod into a tight fibrous rope with a clockwise crank-like motion of his wrists, starting at the top and moving downwards. The rope is looped three times round the bow and under the wale, being kept in tension by continual twisting. Several passages are made like this and the end of the bow rod is roped in too, as illustrated. Both tops are secured by being pulled into the border.

Finally, his work must be dried — outside is best — and the workshop cleared up. There is a day's worth of energy locked into the four baskets and it is hoped that each will take a good ten years of hard use.

ABOVE: *A slewed hamper.*

BELOW: *An oval clothes basket, or 'flasket'.*

ABOVE: *A canvas-covered picnic hamper.*

BELOW: *A fisherman's creel.*

A quarter cran herring basket.

ABOVE: *A bird cage.*
BELOW: *A sandwich box.*

29

A willow chair from Somerset.

ABOVE: *A square provision basket.*
BELOW: *Bushel and half-bushel sieves for fruit, pictured with the basketmaker at Newington, Kent, c 1945. The fruit pickers hanging from the tailboard are called 'kibseys'.*

PLACES TO VISIT

Many museums have a few baskets; those with better collections include the following. Intending visitors are advised to find out the times of opening before making a special journey. Museums marked * hold most of their collection in reserve.

Cambridge and County Folk Museum, 2/3 Castle Street, Cambridge CB3 0AQ. Telephone: Cambridge (0223) 355159.

The Farmland Museum, 50 High Street, Haddenham, Cambridgeshire CB6 3XB. Telephone: Ely (0353) 740381.

Folk Museum, 99-103 Westgate Street, Gloucester GL1 2PG. Telephone: Gloucester (0452) 26467.

Folk Museum of West Yorkshire, Shibden Hall, Halifax, West Yorkshire HX3 6XG. Telephone: Halifax (0422) 52246.

Local History Museum, Little Bolton Town Hall, St Georges Street, Bolton, Lancashire BL1 2EN. Telephone: Bolton (0204) 22311 extension 2192.

Luton Museum and Art Gallery *, Wardown Park, Luton, Bedfordshire LU2 7HA. Telephone: Luton (0582) 36941 or 36942.

Museum of English Rural Life *, The University, Whiteknights, PO Box 229, Reading, Berkshire RG6 2AG. Telephone: Reading (0734) 318660.

Museum of Lincolnshire Life *, The Old Barracks, Burton Road, Lincoln LN1 3LY. Telephone: Lincoln (0522) 28448.

Museum of St Albans, Hatfield Road, St Albans, Hertfordshire AL1 2RR. Telephone: St Albans (0727) 56679.

Newarke Houses Museum *, The Newarke, Leicester LE2 7BY. Telephone: Leicester (0533) 554100 extension 3229.

Norfolk Rural Life Museum, Beech House, Gressenhall, Dereham, Norfolk NR20 4DR. Telephone: Dereham (0362) 860563.

Scottish Fisheries Museum, St Ayles, Harbourhead, Anstruther, Fife KY10 3AB. Telephone: Anstruther (0333) 310628.

Somerset Rural Life Museum, Abbey Farm, Chilkwell Street, Glastonbury, Somerset BA6 8DB. Telephone: Glastonbury (0458) 32903.

Stockwood Craft Museum and Gardens, Stockwood Park, Farley Hill, Luton, Bedfordshire LU1 4BH. Telephone: Luton (0582) 38714.

Welsh Folk Museum *, St Fagans, Cardiff CF5 6XB. Telephone: Cardiff (0222) 569441.

Wigan Pier, Wigan, Lancashire WN3 4EU. Telephone: Wigan (0942) 323666.

Willows and Wetlands Visitor Centre, Meare Green Court, Stoke St Gregory, Taunton, Somerset TA3 6HY. Telephone: Taunton (0823) 490249.

BASKETMAKERS
Stanley Bird Ltd, King Street, Great Yarmouth, Norfolk.
David Drew, Higher Hare Farm, Hare Lane, Buckland St Mary, Chard, Somerset.
John West, 2 Poyle Terrace, Sydenham Road, Guildford, Surrey.

WILLOW SUPPLIERS
P. H. Coate and Son, Meare Green Court, Stoke St Gregory, Taunton, Somerset.
Dereham Brothers, Fosters Farm, North Curry, Taunton, Somerset.
N. Hector, The Willows, Curload, Stoke St Gregory, Taunton, Somerset.
B. Howard, Riverside, Thorney, Langport, Somerset.

FURTHER READING
Bagshawe, T. W. *Basketmaking in Bedfordshire.* Luton Museum and Art Gallery, 1981.
Fitzrandolph, H. E. and Hay, M. D. *The Rural Industries of England and Wales,* volume 2. E P Publishing Ltd, 1977. Historical survey.
Wright, Dorothy. *The Complete Book of Baskets and Basketry.* David and Charles, 1977.